The Flight of the Union

by Tekla White
illustrations by Ralph Ramstad

HISTORY

M Millbrook Press/Minneapolis

Millbrook Press
A division of Lerner Publishing Group, Inc.
241 First Avenue North, Minneapolis, MN 55401 USA

For reading levels and more information,
look up this title at www.lernerbooks.com.

Library of Congress Catologing-in-Publication Data

White, Tekla N.
   The flight of the Union / by Tekla White; illustrations by
Ralph Ramstad.
      p. cm. — (Carolrhoda on my own books)
   Summary: Relates the story of Homan Walsh, a fifteen-year-
old boy who in 1847 successfully flew a kite over the Niagara
River from Canada to the United States, enabling work to
begin on a suspension bridge near Niagara Falls.
   ISBN 978–1–57505–093–5 (lib. bdg. : alk. paper)
   ISBN 978–1–57505–300–4 (pbk. : alk. paper)
   ISBN 978–0–7613–5845–9 (eBook)
   1. Niagara Falls (N.Y. and Ont.)—Fiction. [1. Bridges—
History—Fiction.] I. Ramstad, Ralph, ill. II. Title. III. Series.
PZ7.W584625F1 1998
[Fic]—dc21   97-26687

Manufactured in the United States of America
5 – DOC – 5/1/14

To Jean, Bonny, Theron, and Jeneala.
           —T. W.

*To every young person who has experienced
the dream and the thrill of building a kite
and the pain of losing it.*
           —R. R.

Niagara Falls, New York
March 1847

Homan slowly reeled in his kite.
For weeks, he had worked
to make it strong.
Now he looked it over carefully.
It was the best kite he had ever made.
He hoped it would be strong enough
to win the contest.
The prize was five dollars!
Homan had never even seen
that much money.

Homan had seen posters about
the bridge contest all over town.
He knew that people in the
United States and Canada wanted
to build a bridge
across the Niagara River,
from one country to the other.
To start work on the bridge,
they needed to get a line
across the deep river gorge.

Flying a line across with a kite
was the best way to do it.
They decided to have a contest.
The first person to bring a kite down
on the other side would be the winner.
When Homan heard how the bridge
would bring the two countries together,
he decided to call his kite the Union.
He wanted the Union to be
the kite that started the bridge.

Homan's mother handed him bread
and dried meat wrapped in cloth.
"I may be in Canada a day or two,"
Homan said.
"I'm going to fly the Union
until I have that line in place."
"Remember," his mother said,
"that kite cost me a yard
of my best silk cloth.
I expect it to help build the bridge,
just like you said."
Homan started down the road
to the Niagara River.

The roar of the falls
blocked out all other sounds.
Kite fliers and people who wanted
to watch the contest
crowded into a waiting boat.
Soon it would head for Canada.
The winds usually blew toward
the United States,
so the kites had to be flown
from the Canadian side.

Homan looked over the other kites
on the boat.
Some were bigger than the Union.
But it would take more than size
to win the contest.
How the kite was flown
was also important.
You had to know just the right time
to let the kite drop.

Homan stood next to Mr. Thornton.
"That's a fine kite you have, Homan,"
Mr. Thornton shouted
over the noise of the falls.
"It looks like you have enough string
to fly it to London, England.
I need that bridge so I can buy
more wheat from Canada
for my flour mill.
If you win, I'll match the prize
with five dollars of my own."
"Ten dollars!" Homan whooped.
"Thank you, Mr. Thornton," he said.
"I'll try my best."

The boat passed near
the bottom of the falls.
Cold spray splashed Homan's face.
He covered the Union
with his jacket to keep it dry.

Homan looked up at the towering cliffs
on each side of the river.
He tried to imagine a bridge
hanging in the air,
high above the water.

Before long, the boat docked in Canada.
Along with the other kite fliers,
Homan took the path to the cliff.
They had to walk two miles
to the place where the bridge
would be built.

It looked like every boy in Canada
and the United States wanted
to win the contest.
Homan watched as the sky
filled with kites.
Hundreds of kite tails
waved in the air.

Homan took a deep breath.

Then he tossed the Union up in the air.

It dipped close to the ground,

and Homan pulled it in.

He let out the line again.

This time, the wind held up his kite.

As he let out more line,

Homan thought about his plan.

He would fly the Union

higher than the other kites.

Then his kite could catch the winds
that would blow it across the river.
If Homan flew it too low,
it might smash into the cliffs.
If he let it drop too soon,
it might blow into the water.
He had to keep the Union in the air
until the winds died down.
Then he could bring his kite
down safely.

A small crowd of people came to watch
Homan and the Union.
The kite danced up and down.
Homan could tell that
the high winds weren't steady.
He decided to bring the kite down
and wait for the winds to change.

Two hours later, just before sunset,
Homan saw four of the other kites
flying over the river.
It looked like one of them
might reach the other side.
He couldn't let another kite win.

Homan thought hard,
then he decided.
It was risky,
but he had to take a chance.
He sent the Union sailing up again.
It climbed higher and higher.

Soon it grew dark.

Homan could no longer see his kite.

The air was damp and cold.

Homan pulled his jacket
tightly around him.

No one had gotten a kite across yet,
and the other kites had been reeled in.

"You don't give up, do you?"
said a man holding a lantern.
"The last boat left a long time ago,"
he said, "and you'll need a place
to sleep tonight.
James Barton is the name.
You could keep warm by my fireplace."
"Thank you," answered Homan.

The winds were pulling the Union
toward the water.
The kite could fall in the gorge.
Homan wanted to keep trying,
but he was too tired to hold on
to the kite any longer.
He reeled in the Union
and left with Mr. Barton.

Mr. Barton led the way
along a narrow path.
When they reached the house,
Mrs. Barton hurried them inside.
The table was covered
with bread and bowls of soup.
Homan ate as much as he could
and went to sleep.

The next day, Homan thanked
the Bartons.
Then he headed back to the cliff.
"We'll keep watch for your kite,"
called Mr. Barton.

The Union was the first kite in the air.
By mid-morning,
there were a dozen more.
The southwest wind was steady.
Homan let out rolls and rolls of string.
Finally, the Union was flying
on the other side of the river.

All day, Homan stood with his kite.
Other kites sailed close by.
Homan thought about the prize.
With an extra five dollars
from Mr. Thornton,
he could buy almost anything . . .
maybe even his own horse.

At sunset, some of the kite fliers
gave up and went home.
Most of the people watching left, too.
Then chunks of ice
began crashing down the river.
Homan knew that part of the river
had frozen into ice.
Now the ice had begun
to break into pieces.
Mr. Barton came to the cliff.
"Your kite's on the other side,
but it's not going down," he said.
"You better watch out for that ice."
"The wind will die down," Homan said,
I just have to wait."

At midnight, Homan felt a pull
on the string.
"It's down!" he yelled.
He waited for a signal
from the other side of the river.
Nothing happened.
Suddenly the line felt loose.
"I don't think anyone on the other side
is holding the kite," Homan said.

Mr. Barton tugged at the line.

"It's bad luck, lad," he said.

"The line must have caught
on some ice."

Homan pulled in the broken line.

There was no kite on the end.

The Union was lost!

For the next eight days,
chunks of ice tumbled down the river.
No boats could get across.
Homan stayed with the Bartons.

He walked along the cliff every day,
hoping to see the Union.
But he found only pieces
from other kites.
How would he win the contest now?

When all the ice was finally gone,
Homan took the first boat home.
His mother hugged him
when he came into the house.
"The Union came close
to winning the prize," she said.
"Mr. Thornton found your kite
on the American side."

She handed Homan the Union.

He looked it over.

The frame was cracked in two places.

Part of it was missing.

And it needed a new tail.

Homan wasn't sure he could fix it.

But he knew he had to try.

Homan got right to work.

First he cut new pieces of wood.

Then he carefully attached them

to the silk cloth.

The frame had to be set just right.

Homan tested the kite many times.

After each flight,

he changed the lines and the frame.

Three days passed before
the Union was ready.
Homan took the boat back to Canada.
Only three other boys were still
in the contest.
Homan threw the Union into the air.
Inch by inch, he let out the line.
The wind soon pushed the kite
across the river.

The three other kites flew
close to the Union.
By the end of the day,
two of the kites were down.
One fell into the water.
The other hit the edge of the cliff.
The third kite was bigger
than the Union.
It soared high above Homan's kite.

After a while, Homan's hands
became cramped and cold.
But he held on tight.
One by one, he opened and closed
his fingers.

Now the other boy let out more line.

His kite flew higher,

far away from the water.

It might land safely before Homan

could bring down the Union.

But then the line

on the other kite snapped.

Homan watched the kite disappear.

Now it was up to Homan.

Several farmers came to cheer him on.

In the early evening,

Mr. Barton ran across the clearing.

"Mrs. Barton and I have been watching

the Union all day," he said.

He held up a cup of warm soup.

Homan drank from it without

taking his hands off the line.

It seemed like the winds

were dying down.

Homan thought he felt the line drop.

Then he was sure.

The kite was falling, like it had before.

But this time, Homan saw lanterns
waving on the American side.

He could see the flames of a bonfire.

These signals meant that someone
had won the contest.

One of the farmers shouted,
"We'll take it now, Homan.
Your work is done."
Someone tied down the line.
One end was in Canada and the other
was in the United States!
Homan's kite line was the one
that would help build the bridge.

Everyone was talking and slapping
Homan on the back.
He wanted to shout and run,
but he was too tired to move.
Mr. Barton lifted Homan
to his shoulders.
The noisy crowd followed them
to the Barton farm for a celebration.
Mrs. Barton made special corn cakes
just for Homan.

The next day, Homan took
the boat back home.
Everyone wanted to shake his hand.
When they got to the American side,
Homan saw Mr. Thornton.
He handed Homan his kite
and five silver dollars.
Homan smiled.
He knew that every time
he crossed the new bridge,
he would think of the Union.

Afterword

This story is based on actual events. In the 1840s, people in Canada and the United States wanted to build a bridge across the Niagara River. On August 23, 1846, the Niagara Falls International Bridge Company was formed. A young engineer named Charles Ellet Jr. was chosen to design and build the bridge.

It would be a suspension bridge, so it would hang from cables strung from towers. But before the bridge could be built, Ellet had to find a way to make the first link between Canada and the United States. Someone suggested holding a kite-flying contest.

The day after Homan won the contest in 1847, a rope was attached to the kite line and pulled across the river. When the rope was in place, it was used to pull an iron cable across the river. The cable was then fastened to solid rock. After towers were built on each side of the river, the cable was attached to the towers.

Next, the builders needed a way to carry people and supplies from one side of the river to the other. They decided to build an iron basket with room for two people and some supplies. The basket hung from a cable and could be pulled from one side to the other.

The Niagara Falls Suspension Bridge was opened on August 1, 1848. Near Niagara Falls today, six bridges join the United States and Canada. Trains, cars, and trucks move quickly from one country to the other. Homan Walsh will be remembered as the person who made the first link.

48